# _Why Do You Stare?_

# _A Reflection of Me Through Poetry_

## _By Angelica Henderson_

Maynetre Manuscripts, LLC
Florida

ISBN Number: 0-985-44636-6 (Paperback)
ISBN Number: 0-985-44637-4 (eBook)
LCCN: 2013942599

Why Do You Stare? A Reflection of Me Through Poetry
Copyright © 2013 Angelica Henderson
Published by Maynetre Manuscripts, LLC
*Writing To Right The Broken Soul*

All rights reserved. Except for use in the case of brief quotations embodied in critical articles and reviews, the reproduction or utilization of this work in whole or part in any form by any electronic, digital, mechanical or other means, now known or hereafter invented, including xerography, photocopying, scanning, recording, or any information storage or retrieval system, is forbidden without written prior permission of the author and publisher, Maynetre Manuscripts, LLC.

The scanning, uploading, and distribution of this book via the Internet or via any other means without permission of the publisher and author is illegal and punishable by law. Purchase only authorized versions of this book, and do not participate in or encourage electronic piracy of copyrighted materials. Your support of the author's rights is appreciated.

This is a work of fiction. Names, characters, places, and incidents are products of the author's imagination, the author's own personal experience, or are used fictitiously and are not to be construed as real. While the author was inspired in part by actual events, the characters are not distantly inspired by any individual known or unknown to the author. Any resemblance to actual events, locales, business establishments, organizations, or persons, living or dead, is entirely coincidental.

Printed in the United States of America
First Printing 2013
10 9 8 7 6 5 4 3 2 1

Edited by: Shantae A. Charles for God Ideas, LLC www.shantaecharles.org
& Cynthia M. Lamb www.lambeditorial.webs.com
Cover Design: ROC Studios International, Inc.

## Dedication Prayer

God, I thank you for waking me up this morning and starting me on my way. I bless Your Name, for there is nothing and/or no one greater than You. Lord, you sent your Angels to watch over me once again. You said in your word that you would never leave me nor forsake me, and I thank you for being with me always, even now.

Lord, I pray you would minister to those who will read the words on these pages. I pray that you would send your Holy Spirit to minister to them. I pray that my prose will change lives for the better. I pray that my words will inspire people like never before.

Lord, I thank you for allowing me to write this book and bring this work to completion. I may receive recognition from the world, but Lord, I pray that I will never become so engrossed in fame that I fail to acknowledge You. I pray that this work of literature will be a blessing to the world.

I thank you for all that You have done, all that You are doing, and what You will continue to do in my life. I know that You are more than able to do exceedingly, abundantly and above all that I am able to ask or think. Your ways are not my ways and Your thoughts are higher than my thoughts. There is no limit to what You can do; so I dedicate this work to You. I thank you for hearing, answering, and going beyond this prayer, in Jesus Name, Amen.

## **Acknowledgements**

First, I would like to thank God for being the head of my life. I thank God for sending His Holy Spirit to be a comforter to me and to inspire me. None of this would be possible without Him.

I would like to thank my parents, Robert and Alicia Henderson for everything. I love you so much Mom and Dad. I would like to thank my sisters, Ashley and Jasmine Henderson. I thank God for you, and I thank God that he blessed me with two wonderful sisters. I love you both very much.

I would like to thank Maynetre Manuscripts, LLC - Tallahassee, FL - for publishing this book. I appreciate Tremayne Moore for believing in me enough to give me such an opportunity as this one. I would also like to thank Shantae A. Charles for taking the time out to preview and edit my work. I appreciate your feedback and constructive criticism. I would like to thank Robert O. Charles for designing my book cover and to Cynthia M. Lamb for copy-editing and proofreading my work.

I would like to thank Darrell D. Kelly (Free Spirit Community Church) – Panama City, FL, for all you have done for me. I thank you for speaking into my life. I thank you for allowing God to use you to minister to me and teach me all of the things that you have taught me. You have always challenged me to do better. You are also one of the few people who accept me for who I am, and you constantly remind me that it is ok to be "different." I remember the first time I saw you playing the keyboard at Free Spirit. I have always dreamed of being able to minister to people like you do. I have been blessed with the ability and opportunity to do just that. You inspire me, and I appreciate you so much.

I would like to thank the following churches for all that you have done for me and for allowing me to serve in various ministries: Love & Worship Center Church of the Living God (Apostle Shirley C. White & Bishop Daniel White) - Apalachicola, FL; New Beginnings Assembly of the Saints Church (Pastor Lonnie and Pastor Marion Mitchell) - Panama City, FL; Free Spirit Community Church (Apostle James & Pastor Margie Kelly) - Panama City, FL; Living Word International Ministries (Bishop Clarence and Lady Wanda Williams) - Junction City, KS; Destiny Christian Center (Dr. Jessie and Pastor Halene Giddens) - Victorville, CA; and Harvest Family Church (Dr. E.B and Dr. Rosa Herman) - Fayetteville, NC.

# Table of Contents

**I. Opening Statement**
- A Generation My Generation ............................................. 7
- Welcome To My World ..................................................... 8
- WATCH THIS ................................................................... 9
- What's Your Slant? ......................................................... 10

**II. Enough Is Enough**
- The Two of Us ................................................................ 11
- Constant Reminders (Parts 1 & 2) .................................. 13
- My Divorce ..................................................................... 15
- Why Do You Stare? (Remix) ........................................... 16
- The Commandments for Taking Your Life Back ............. 17
- What's Your Slant? ......................................................... 18

**III. Written Thoughts**
- My P.D.A. ....................................................................... 19
- Anonymous Thanks ........................................................ 20
- Patrick ............................................................................ 21
- Here I Lay ...................................................................... 22
- You Are My Everything .................................................. 23
- Recognition .................................................................... 24
- What's Your Slant? ......................................................... 25

**IV. Deception**
- My True Friend. ............................................................. 26
- 1st Time, 2nd Time ........................................................ 27
- Text Message ................................................................. 28
- What's Your Slant? ......................................................... 29

## V. Exclusive

Present, Past and Future ............................................................ 30

Hide And Go Seek ...................................................................... 31

Last Night ................................................................................... 34

Seen And Unseen ....................................................................... 35

Live To Serve .............................................................................. 36

What's Your Slant? ..................................................................... 37

## VI. Fulfillment

ROYALTY. ................................................................................... 38

A Man vs. A Boy ......................................................................... 39

Spoken Eyes ............................................................................... 40

Complete And Satisfied ............................................................. 41

Elijah James-Robert ................................................................... 42

New Day ..................................................................................... 43

I Do .............................................................................................. 44

What's Your Slant? ..................................................................... 45

**About The Author** .......................................................................... 46

Why Do You Stare? A Reflection of Me Through Poetry

# I. Opening Statement

## **A Generation, My Generation**

In this world that I live in, it never ceases to amaze me
With my heart, with my eyes I continually see
A generation, my generation
Of young people in desperate need

From the clothes and the shoes
To the hair and tattoos
I never understood why being your own self
You never choose.
Instead you substitute expression for duplication
And imitation
Thinking you're hip and not simply
Media's fools

Ladies, you are unique and special
Males, you have so much potential
We have to do better for
Things to get better

Ladies, you have the key
Ladies, you set the standard
If he loves you, he will be ready to handle all that you require of him
He will appreciate you for who you are
And not for what you can do for him

Men take care of their babies; they don't make us go it alone
If you don't want us for real, then play house at your own home

Ladies, stop the arguing, stop the fighting
This is not attractive and it's definitely not inviting
I understand the hurt –trust me; I understand the pain
But we have to let it go. Forgive
Let it roll down like rain

In this world that I live in, it never ceases to amaze me
With my heart, with my eyes I continually see
A generation, my generation, of young people in desperate need

## **Welcome To My World**

I woke up this morning, and I looked to my left. There was no one there by my side. I looked at my fingers, and there were only two rings on the right side.
I looked at my room. There were no babies for me.
There was no one to send to school, no diapers to change, and no mouths to feed.
I looked at my keys. There was no reason to make them wake.
There was no work for me. There was no earthly income to be made.
I looked at my instruments; I found they were limited.
Music is in me, but there were no CDs to be printed.
I closed my eyes, and I began to meditate.
I was not alone. I have been with God all day.
He allowed me to see (with my natural eyes) my world.
Now, I can share this with you and bring you into my world.
So, I felt like writing, and it is after two.
Now, I am sharing this with you.

Welcome to my world.
Hear the DJ spinning?
All the beats are Mine
And the lyrics say,
Winning, Winning, Winning.

## **WATCH THIS**

God woke me up this morning. He is the reason why I live.
Today I have the use and activity of my limbs.
He said, "Get Up," and I did that. "Put your glasses on," and I did that.
"Wash your face, comb your hair, take your medicine," and I did that.
God blessed me with a Hyundai; forget your Rolls-Royce.
God blessed me; I am a blessing; so mine is better than yours.
Forget your top back, your Maybach music, and your suicide butterfly doors.
I have the sunroof, the tinted windows, and the manufactured speakers.
The sound is so clear. I do not need those stupid boom-boom bass speakers.
My face is so pretty. You can't tell what it has been through.
Look into my eyes. "You Are Beautiful."
You can't tell how it can relate to you unless I told you.
You say that you love me; you can upgrade me.
You say that you want me, and I am so pretty.
But if you will not be the for real truth, keep it moving.
DON'T TALK TO ME!!!

## What's Your Slant?

Who do you think each poem within the "Opening Statement" section is written to?

What pictures come to your mind as you read each poem in this section?

What's your favorite line (s) in each poem within this section?

If you had to add another stanza to each poem within this section, what would you write?

Other Thoughts

___
___
___
___
___
___
___
___
___
___
___
___
___

## II. Enough Is Enough

# **<u>The Two of Us</u>**

One, Two, Three, Four
I don't want to do this anymore.
Five, Six, Seven, Eight
I have to go. I will not wait.
One, Two, Three, Four
Our son and I head for the door.
Five, Six, Seven, Eight
It's over. I'm done—Who cares what's at stake?

One, Two, Three, Four
My scarred hand reaches for the door.
Five, Six, Seven, Eight
You grab me, and I hear you say, "Baby, please wait! Listen to me, I can explain."
Personally, I don't want to hear your futile lies, but for my baby (your son's sake), my heart wants to know, though it's breaking inside.

I know...I hear you plead, "Don't turn around!" I hear you. My baby is crying. "Run Away!" I'm trying.

One, Two, Three, Four
I don't want to do this anymore.
You say that you will not hurt me anymore.
You say that you will curse me no more.
You say that you won't leave me anymore.
You say that you will see her no more.
You say that you won't hit me no more.
You say that you will blame me no more.
You say that if I leave, then you can't love anymore.
Look at me now, I am out the door.
Five, Six, Seven, Eight

"I'm Sorry" is too late.

Hitting the road?
That's me,
You've hit me enough
Ha! I *know* God would agree!
I'm not taking any flack
No, I'll never be back
No more, No More, No More, No More.
You've had your *last* wrestling match
I'll never be back No More.

Why Do You Stare? A Reflection of Me Through Poetry

# **Constant Reminders (Parts 1 & 2)**

(Part 1)

My name is Amy.
I am constantly reminded that I need to be pretty for a man in this world to see me.

My name is Terry.
I am constantly reminded that I am not married.

My name is Cassandra.
I am constantly reminded of the drama.

My name is Wanda.
I am constantly reminded that I am five-foot one.

My name is Shawn.
I am constantly reminded that I still live at home with my mom.

My name is Barbara.
I am constantly reminded that I was born first, the oldest one.

My name is Katie.
I am constantly reminded that I do not drive a Mercedes.

My name is Jamie.
I am constantly reminded that I still have not given birth to a baby.

My name is Susie.
I am constantly reminded of his bruises.

My name is Judy.
I am constantly reminded that you are a dead-beat dad. Loser.

My name is Sophie.
I am constantly reminded that you continue to leave me.

My name is Toni.
I am constantly reminded that I don't have much money.

## Why Do You Stare? A Reflection of Me Through Poetry

My name is Mary Jo.
I am constantly reminded of this military life, and I don't have a place to call home.

My name is Flo.
I am constantly reminded that my Ex was on the Down Low, Homosexual.

(Part 2)

Remember that I am more than just a pretty face.
Never forget that God is still in love with me.
Remember that my past is erased.
Never forget that I do not take up much space.
Remember that I can live on my own, and I don't need you to feed me.
Never forget that I was born a leader.
Remember that it was God who blessed me with a Hyundai.
Never forget that I will have a baby, just not before I am married.
Remember that he did not break me.
Never forget that he is still the father of my baby.
Remember that God is always with me.
Never forget that I work hard for my money.
Remember that I was born into this military life.
Never forget that no matter how low men stoop
Remember that with God you can leap over troops.
Never forget that I divorced him, and he is out of my life.
Remember that I am still a keeper, an excellent wife.

## **My Divorce**

Every person who has hurt me in any way, I am letting them go.
Every thing that has caused me pain, I am letting them go.
Every idea that has produced no gain, I am letting them go.
Every scar that continues to look the same, I am letting them go.

Every negative word that was said to me, I am letting them go.
Every lie that was told to me, I am letting them go.
Every man who has attempted to break me, I am letting them go.
Everything that is not satisfying, I am letting them go.

Every doctor who has said that there was no cure, I am letting them go.
Every thought that was not pure, I am letting them go.
Every stupid lecture that I had to endure, I am letting them go.
Every time I was ignored, I am letting them go.

Every prescription drug that made me worse, I am letting them go.
Every time I was coerced, I am letting them go.
Every achievement that I have earned, and you took the credit as yours, I am letting them go.
Every taker who stole from my purse, I am letting them go.

This is my decree, my bill of divorce from the negative impulses I was tied to, bound to, married to, and in union with. From here on out, you are free from me, and I am free from you!

Why Do You Stare? A Reflection of Me Through Poetry

## **<u>Why Do You Stare? (Remix)</u>**

Why do you stare?
Is it because I am different from you?
Is it because I do not look like you?

Why do you stare?
Is it because of my hopes...my dreams my...determination?
Is it because of what I am facing?

Why do you stare?
Is it because I have multiple piercings in my ear?
Is it because I always persevere?

Why do you stare?
Is it because my stature is petite?
Is it because my personality is quite unique?

Why do you stare?
Is it because I was diagnosed with Guillain-Barre' Syndrome?
Is it because I do not have a smart phone?

Why do you stare?
Is it because I live with Jesus outside of church?
Is it because I stay with him for better and worse?

Why do you stare?
Is it because of all of my accomplishments?
Is it because you only want me to share it?

Why do you stare?
Is it because I am in a loving relationship with him?
Is it because you always wish that you were him?

Why do you stare?
Is it because I try new styles with my hair?
Is it because every for opinion you have of me I really do not care?
Why do you stare?
Is it because you cannot accept me?
Is it because no matter what, you will respect me?

## **The Commandments for Taking Your Life Back**

You will not make me cry anymore.
You will not yell at me anymore.
You will not lie to me anymore.
You will not cause me not to tell anymore.

You will not pull my hair anymore.
You will not cheat on me anymore.
You will not act like you do not care anymore.
You will not deceive me anymore.

You will not verbally abuse me anymore.
You will not break my phone anymore.
You will not financially use me anymore.
You will not make me feel alone anymore.

You will not slap my face anymore.
You will not come to my house anymore.
You will not spit in my face anymore.
You will not ask me out anymore.

You will not visit my employer anymore.
You will not take my joy anymore.
You will not call my lawyer anymore.
You will not exploit me anymore.

## What's Your Slant?

Who do you think each poem within the "Enough Is Enough" section is written to?

What pictures come to your mind as you read each poem in this section?

What's your favorite line (s) in each poem within this section?

If you had to add another stanza to each poem within this section, what would you write?

Other Thoughts

_____
_____
_____
_____
_____
_____
_____
_____
_____
_____
_____
_____
_____

## III. Written Thoughts

## <u>My P.D.A.</u>

I want to tell you about a man that I know.
He is wonderful. He compliments me so.
I am attracted to him so much.
When we talk, I am nervous.

He makes me smile...I love it.
Our personalities match; I love it.
He is smart, and kind, and funny, all in one.
He is genuine and real; this is awesome.

He invites me; he excites me.
I admire him; he respects me.

I want to see his face.
I want to know his warm embrace.
Separated by location, why so much space?
I just had to tell someone about this man that I know.

## **Anonymous Thanks**

Thank you for introducing yourself to me.
Thank you for helping me at the vending machine.
Thank you for talking to me.
Thank you for going to the movies.
Thank you for calling me.
Thank you for listening.
Thank you for not judging me when you found out about my virginity.
Thank you for laughing with me instead of laughing at me.
Thank you for being a friend to me.

Why Do You Stare? A Reflection of Me Through Poetry

## **Patrick**

I remember when I first met you, that day was so special to me.
Your smile was like none I had ever seen.
It took my breath away when I saw your smile.
My heart melted and my soul smiled.
I took you out of your car seat and embraced you.
You kissed me, and I knew I would enjoy being around you.
I sat you on my lap, and we talked for a few; our relationship grew.
I had a chance to spend some quality time with you.

I discovered some things within the first week of caring for you that I don't think they, your parents, even knew.
You love music, you are strong, and you don't cry much.
You have the ability to calm a room, and you don't even say much.
You are smart. You have good, soft and curly baby hair.
To some people that seems unfair.
I cannot fail to mention you are left-handed.

I cared for you just like you were one of my own.
You were a joy to have in my home.
We ate lunch together; we went to the park together.
And when you cried, I was there to make it all better.
I held you in my arms close to me and began to sing to you, all better.

I think about you often, for we became close.
Our level of trust is what I admire most.
Even though you have to go home now, you will always be with me.
Forever in my heart is where you will be.
So, I will see you later, and I hope that you remember me.

## **Here I Lay**

I am awake, and it is four minutes after one in the morning.
It is cold outside. I think that it might be snowing.
I lay here and meditate on all that God has done.
Excuse me for a moment while He and I have this conversation:
God, you woke me up yesterday and started me on my way.
You allowed me to go to work. I had a great day.
Lord, your mercies are new to me daily.
What my heart feels is amazing.
You said in your word that you would never leave me.
You said in your word that you would never forsake me.
God, I pray that it will always be more of you and less of me.
I pray that your people will see you through me.

## **You Are My Everything**

Lord, You are awesome.
Lord, You hear me when I call.
Lord, You never let me fall.
You are my everything.

Lord, You are my Father.
Lord, You are my provider.
Lord, You are my healer.
Lord, You are my teacher.
You are my everything.

Lord, You are my shelter.
Lord, You are my protector.
Lord, You are my deliverer.
Lord, You are my Savior.
You are my everything.

Lord, You are majestic.
Lord, You are infinite.
Lord, You are angelic.
You are my everything.

Lord, You are Holy.
Lord, I put no one before thee.
Lord, You are my King.
You are my everything.

Lord, You are jealous.
Lord, You are precious.
Lord, Your spirit is contagious.
Lord, You are amazing.
You are my everything.

## **Recognition**

The entire room is silent. Everyone is quiet.
All eyes are on me as my heart races.
Listen to what you are telling me as I read all of your faces:
"Who is this girl? What does she have to say? Why should I care anyway?"
My nervousness is alive.
Fear instigates, "Go ahead, just run and hide."
I close my eyes and breathe before I begin to speak.
Your anticipation is talking to me.
I can feel my legs shake, and it seems like an earthquake.
No one is bored and wondering how long this will take.
Today I receive recognition.
I open my mouth, and then you receive recognition.

## What's Your Slant?

Who do you think each poem within the "Written Thoughts" section is written to?

What pictures come to your mind as you read each poem in this section?

What's your favorite line (s) in each poem within this section?

If you had to add another stanza to each poem within this section, what would you write?

Other Thoughts

_____
_____
_____
_____
_____
_____
_____
_____
_____
_____
_____
_____
_____
_____
_____
_____
_____

## IV. Deception

## <u>My True Friend</u>

I Opened Myself Up to You
I Wanted to Be Your Friend
Instead You Played These Mind Games
That Seemed to Never End

You Brought Him In
To Add Fuel to The Fire
Which With Me He Tried to Fulfill
His Own Lust and Desire

Using Two Phones He Tried to Spit Game
Trying to Be You
When Really He Was the Same

You Thought You Had Me
You Thought I Fell for the Lies
But Yet You Failed to Realize
This Just Focused My Eyes
On The One Who Gives Me
Joy and Peace

Jesus is My True Friend
Which is Something
You Will NEVER!
EVER!
EVER!
Be.

# 1st Time, 2nd Time

The 1st Time,
You Left Me.
The 2nd Time,
You Never Came Back.

The 1st Time,
You Hurt Me.
The 2nd Time,
You Never Made It Better.

The 1st Time,
You Deceived Me.
The 2nd Time,
I Was Blind-Sided.

The 1st Time,
You Lied To Me.
The 2nd Time,
I Found Out From Someone Else.

After What You Did To Me
How Can My Negative
Become My Positive?

The 1st Time,
You Made Me Strong.
The 2nd Time,
You Made Me Unbreakable!

## **Text Message**

I went online to check my messages, and I was surprised
Shocked, really to see one addressed to me from *you*?
It's been a while since I set my eyes on your face.
I opened your letter, my heart racing.
One emotion pounding the others into dust: total anticipation.
Your greeting starts out with a nice "Hello."
But I know you; so I am wondering where this will go.
To my surprise, you were quite the gentleman.
Towards the end, you wanted to know when you could see me again.
We went out for a while, and you called me daily.
Is this serious? I don't know, *maybe*?

One day I went Christmas shopping for you with some friends.
We all rode in one car to the outside mall in San Destin.
I went into the Nike store and bought you a pair of shoes and a hat.
I know your style; so I know you will like that.
It's getting cold outside. Night's breeze kisses my nose.
It's late; so we head back home.
I can't wait to get back and tell you how my day went.
Next thing I know, I received a text message from you wanting me to meet your girlfriend.

Now I know I was nothing to you
A call for convenience
A text message Boo.

## What's Your Slant?

Who do you think each poem within the "Deception" section is written to?

What pictures come to your mind as you read each poem in this section?

What's your favorite line (s) in each poem within this section?

If you had to add another stanza to each poem within this section, what would you write?

Other Thoughts

_____
_____
_____
_____
_____
_____
_____
_____
_____
_____
_____
_____
_____
_____

## V. Exclusive

## **Present, Past and Future**

PRESENTLY
I Am Running From A Hurtful And Painful
PAST
Trying To Reach What Some People Call
A Seemingly Unrealistic
FUTURE
Which I Am Trying To Make My PRESENT Reality
I Have Been Rejected
So Many Times Before
But I Still Want To Be The Best
So I Stop At Nothing To Touch Success

## **Hide And Go Seek**

There is a party going on, and all of the adults are downstairs.
There is a party going on, and I am upstairs.
We are watching TV, and everyone is so carefree.
One of the boys says, "Let's play Hide and Go Seek."

So, we all formed a circle to see who would be "It."
One. Two. Three. I am not "It."
She begins to count, and we all start to scatter.
I found the best hiding place, but that does not matter.

I open the door and go into the poolroom.
I am hiding in the closet that is in this room.
I am so quiet. I know she will not find me.
Then he opens the door-- how did *you* find me?

I tell him to get out, but he puts his hand over my mouth.
I am screaming so hard, but nothing is coming out.
I break myself free, and I start running.
The door is locked from the outside. What will happen to me?

He comes out of the closet as he follows me.
I turn and look into his eyes. He is angry.
He starts to laugh at me.
He says, "You are scared of me."

"This game is over. I am not playing anymore."
"Leave me alone. I will tell you no more. Get over here and open this door."
He says, "You are not going anywhere."
"Now, come over here, and do not make me come over there."

He grabs my arm and pulls me close.

## Why Do You Stare? A Reflection of Me Through Poetry

I try to push away, and he tears my clothes.
I begin to cry. He sees the tears fall.
He is not fazed as he slams me into the wall.

He says to me, "You better kiss me."
I refuse and turnd my head as his fist barely misses me.
I tell him to let me go, but he says, "No."
"Let's find out which way this will go..."

Fast forward this a little bit; I promise to make it quick.
Try not to blink; for if you do, you will miss this.

He slams me onto the pool table. I am now on my back.
He is holding my wrists down, and there is no way to fight back.
To him, the fear in my eyes is priceless.
I try to kick him away, but he finds this enticing.

"Tell me that you love me."
I tell him "No."
"Tell me that you love me."
I tell him "No."

All of a sudden, the atmosphere becomes clear.
He pulls me up from the table, and my face is still filled with fear.
I wish this all could have been a dream.
I made the mistake and screamed.

"Do you love me?" I said, "No."
Now, I am starring at the ground as he holds me by the neck out of the second story window.
I cried to him, "Please don't let me go!"
He says, "I will pull you back up if you tell me you love me."
I tell him I love him as my eyes beg him not to drop me.

He pulls me back up and turns me around. Now he is standing behind me.

Why Do You Stare? A Reflection of Me Through Poetry

He whispers in my ear, "that's a good girl," as he wraps his arms around me.
My body quivers. The teardrops fall from my eyes and hit the carpet.
He says, "If you tell anyone, I'll bring you back in here and finish what I started."

The game is over now. It is ok to come out of the room.
He went and sat on the couch, but I went and cried in the bathroom.
I wanted to go home.
A few hours later our moms came to get us, and we all went home.

I was too afraid to say anything to anyone that night.
But a few years later, he and his daughter's mother got into a physical fight.
He beat her so bad that she went to the hospital. He went to jail.
As for me, God blessed me to live, and now I have a story to tell.

## Last Night

It was a chaotic night at my house last night.
People came in and out of my house last night.
The music was blasting all night last night.
People were dancing, drinking and smoking last night.
I wanted to leave so bad last night.
But I had nowhere else to go last night.
Plus I had the baby last night.
Food was all over the floor last night.
The Vodka was in my refrigerator last night.
The people did not care last night.
They were passed out everywhere last night.
There was even a girl asleep in my bathtub last night.
There were clothes all over the floor last night.
And the shoes left my carpet stained last night.
I stayed in my room last night.
I also had to do laundry last night.
I could not sleep last night.
I was surprised that the baby did not wake up last night.
I saw his Dad for a minute last night.
He was with his people last night.
He had to work last night.
I finally fell asleep last night.
I slept for two hours last night.
Through it all, God was still with me last night.
And He sent his Angels to watch over me last night.

## **Seen And Unseen**

What you do see is this smile on my face.
What you don't see are his bruises on my face.
What you do see is his affection towards me.
What you don't see is him abusing me.

What you do see are these jackets and long sleeves.
What you don't see is what these hospital treatments do to me.
What you do see is a small stomach.
What you don't see is how most foods make me vomit.

What you do see are these clothes.
What you don't see are these holes.
What you do see is my heart, which is genuine and true.
What you don't see is me like you.

## **Live To Serve**

I am on this stage every week, and it is amazing to me what I see.
As I begin to play, the Holy Spirit takes control over me.
God ministers through me.
I never look at your faces, for they are always filled with judgment.
Stop looking at me, and put your focus on the One by whom I'm sent.

His glory is what you should see when you look at me.
I pray that you see more of Him and less of me.
People constantly compliment me on how well I play these instruments.
Please understand that this music that is in me is a gift.

I always meditate and pray before I come before you.
I pray for God to minister through me to you.
I am a chosen vessel with a will to serve.
I glorify God and give Him the praise that only He deserves.

When you see me on stage, know that I am not doing this for you.
I am not looking for any type of approval from you.
As long as God is pleased with me, other opinions are mere chatter.
At the end of the day, if God has been magnified, then that is all that matters.

## What's Your Slant?

Who do you think each poem within the "Exclusive" section is written to?

What pictures come to your mind as you read each poem in this section?

What's your favorite line (s) in each poem within this section?

If you had to add another stanza to each poem within this section, what would you write?

Other Thoughts

_____
_____
_____
_____
_____
_____
_____
_____
_____
_____
_____
_____
_____
_____

## VI. Fulfillment

### *ROYALTY*

He Treats Me Like A Queen
This Man That I Know
I Don't Have To Worry
Degrading Language I Will Never Know

His Speech Is Articulate
He Speaks With Conviction
And I Will Not Hesitate To Mention
He Can Sing

He's A Listener Whenever It's Needed
Always Caring, Always Understanding, Never Deceitful
His Honesty Is Appreciated, Never Taken For Granted
Whether To Trust Is Not An Issue

He Accepts Me For Who I Am
Games He Does Not Play
And What Can I Say
That Is What Has Always Been Wanted

He Knows How To Love
I Know That It's Heaven Sent
With Him It Is Alright; I Am Content

I Will Continue To Learn And Grow
Who Knows What The Outcome Will Be
We Will Just Wait And See...

## **A Man vs. A Boy**

A Man Understands The Game
A Boy Plays The Game
A Man Knows What He Wants
A Boy Is Confused

A Man Has A Purpose For His Life
A Boy Is Still Searching
A Man Overcomes His Past
A Boy Is Still Hurting

A Man Fathers His Children
A Boy Makes Babies
A Man Is Definite
A Boy Settles For "Maybe"

A Man Protects His Relationship
A Boy Runs Away From One
A Man Will Comfort A Broken Heart
A Boy Will Continue To Break One

A Man Is In Love With You
A Boy Loves What You Can Do
A Man Is Honest With You
A Boy Is Half-Honest To Get You

## **Spoken Eyes**

Look into my eyes, and what will you see?
You will see a beautiful girl.
You will see that I want you in my world.

Look into my eyes, and what will you see?
You will see a heart that wants to love you.
You will see that I smile when I am around you.

Look into my eyes, and what will you see?
You will see that I am blessed and highly favored.
You will see that Jesus Christ is my Lord and Savior.

Look into my eyes, and what will you see?
You will see that because of you, there is no one else for me.
You will see that I am complete.

Look into my eyes and what will you see?
You will see that I am genuine.
You will see that I am alive.

## **Complete And Satisfied**

There is something different about this atmosphere.
This atmosphere is calm, and it is clear.
It is clear to me that you truly love me.
You truly love me, and you are the one for me.
For me, this is real love.
Real love is all that I have wanted.
I have wanted to know what this felt like for so long.
For so long, I have wanted to be with you.
With you, I am complete.
Complete And Satisfied.

## **Elijah James-Robert**

You are so beautiful to me.
You are a joy to me.
Your smile is so amazing to me.
Your kisses are so warming to me.

Your presence lights up any room.
Your laughter changes the entire mood.
Your cries are never rude.
I am always there to comfort you.

Throughout the night, I hold you close.
My warm embrace is the one that you know.
My smile is the one that you admire most.
I love you more than you will ever know.

I would like for you to meet my son.
His presence needs no introduction.
He is a little of me, a creation from God.
He is the joy of my soul.
He is the warmth of my heart.

## New Day

Today is a brand new day.
I woke up this morning with a smile on my face.
Today is a good day.
I declare that things will go my way according to God's way.
I have life and life more abundantly.
My friend called me just to say "hey."
Another one invited me over for the weekend to stay.
I went out to dinner, and I did not even have to pay.
God favors me; what more can I say?
I went to work today and received a pay raise.
Do you see what God will do when you back off and let him have His way?
I always put Him first everyday.
I meditate, praise, worship, and pray.
I read His word and apply it to my life daily.
I walk by faith and not by maybe.
Today is a brand new day.

## **I Do**

As I put on this dress right now, I cannot explain all that my heart feels.
All of this seems so surreal.
I have decided to take this next step with you.
I vow to give all of my love to you.

You have always been there for me even in the midnight hour.
Our conversations sometimes continue hour after hour.
You always encourage me, never belittling.
I have allowed you to see me like no one else has seen.
I can be vulnerable with you, and you will never take advantage of me.

You take time to listen to what I have to say.
You have a smile that always brightens up my day.
You know my strengths, but you still help me anyway.
And when I seem at a loss, you always remind me to pray.

You have done so much for me when no one else did.
Most importantly, you are my best friend.
I have been patiently waiting for this treasured time.
To make it official, to hear you say, "You're mine."

## What's Your Slant?

Who do you think each poem within the "Fulfillment" section is written to?

What pictures come to your mind as you read each poem in this section?

What's your favorite line (s) in each poem within this section?

If you had to add another stanza to each poem within this section, what would you write?

Other Thoughts

_____
_____
_____
_____
_____
_____
_____
_____
_____
_____
_____
_____
_____
_____
_____

## About The Author

Angelica Alicia Henderson was born in Frankfurt, Germany. She arrived to the United States (Oklahoma) in 1989 and has lived in the States ever since. She has lived in various states including: Oklahoma, Florida, California, North Carolina, Georgia, Kansas, and South Carolina.

God has blessed Angelica with various gifts and talents including, but not limited to: writing, reading music, singing, producing music, signing language, and playing a variety of instruments. Singing since the age of five, Angelica's passion resides strongly with music, for which she holds an Associate of Arts degree in Music and is currently working on a Bachelor of Science degree in Music Production.

Angelica currently serves at Harvest Family Church in the role of a Musician, under the leadership of Dr. E.B. & Dr. Rosa Herman. She is committed to helping people and sharing her gifts with the world at large.

www.ingramcontent.com/pod-product-compliance
Lightning Source LLC
Chambersburg PA
CBHW031437040426
42444CB00006B/857